W9-BAJ-045

THE KEY TO ART

THE KEY TO PAINTING

Juan-Ramón Triadó
Professor of Art History

Lerner Publications Company • Minneapolis

Copyright ©1988 Editorial Planeta, Spain

Copyright © 1990 English language, David Bateman Ltd.

This edition published 1990
by Lerner Publications Company
241 First Avenue North, Minneapolis, Minnesota 55401, USA

In association with David Bateman Ltd.
32-34 View Road, Glenfield, Auckland, New Zealand

All rights to this edition reserved. International copyright secured. No part of this book may be reproduced or transmitted in any form or by any means, electronic or mechanical, including photocopying and recording, or by any information storage or retrieval system without the prior written permission of the publisher except for the inclusion of brief quotations in an acknowledged review.

LIBRARY OF CONGRESS CATALOGING-IN-PUBLICATION DATA

Triadó, Juan-Ramón.
[Claves de la pintura. English]
The key to painting/Juan-Ramón Triadó.
p. cm.—(The Key to art)
Translation of: Las claves de la pintura.

Includes index.
Summary: Traces, through text and color plates, the history of painting, from early cave paintings to those of the twentieth century. Discusses the history of the artist's tools and the use of technique, perspective, proportion, and compositon.
ISBN 0-8225-2050-8 (lib. bdg.)
ISBN 0-8225-2053-2 (pbk.)
1. Composition (Art) 2. Painting—Technique. [1. Composition (Art) 2. Painting—Technique. 3. Art appreciation.] I. Title. II. Series.
ND1475.T7513 1990
750'.1—dc20 89-12233
CIP
AC

A David Bateman Book

Printed in Spain
Bound in USA by Muscle Bound Bindery

1 2 3 4 5 6 7 8 9 10 99 98 97 96 95 94 93 92 91 90

INTRODUCTION

Painting is the visual art form best known to most of us. If you ask anyone to name a few painters, sculptors, and architects, most of those listed will be painters. We know their names from the great collections in art galleries and museums. Very often, however, we appreciate the fame of the artist rather than the real beauty of the work. Paintings, more than other works of art, must be appreciated for their form, meaning, and content.

Some knowledge of composition theory helps those trying to understand and appreciate a painting. It also helps to understand the conditions, as well as the time and place, in which the painting was created.

PAUL CÉZANNE. *The Card Players*. 1890-95. Musée d'Orsay, Paris, France.
The basic value of **form**, or design, is clear in this picture. Cézanne's paintings lack any extra decoration. They keep closely to what he considered essential—a sense of geometry, or the arrangement of parts. Yet, his works always give the viewer much to think about.

Abstract art, where form and color are more important than the subject, has greatly increased our understanding of painting styles. A painting should not be judged by its subject, but by the balance it achieves

ANONYMOUS, ITALIAN. *The Martyrdom of Saint Andrew*. End of 17th century. Diocesan Museum, Lerida, Spain. Though the name of the painter of this magnificent work is unknown, he or she was certainly a great artist. Here we can appreciate a painting without knowing its creator. We can value and analyze the work itself. A painter becomes a **master**—an artist whose work is a model or an ideal—when he or she creates a new form of expression and maintains an overall high standard for a period of time.

between form and content. Abstract art gets ideas across through shape, as well as line and color.

Our appreciation for the arts is firmly rooted in our feelings. Our personal tastes usually cause us to like or to dislike a painting. However, enjoying a picture intellectually gives us a richer and less-biased appreciation. Try to avoid being influenced by ideas or feelings associated with the subject of the painting.

Visual understanding of a painting must be based on the idea that form has meaning. Many critics emphasize this fact. They talk about the life of form, the spirit and the content of significant form. These ideas are important to any work of art.

Throughout this book we shall see that form has great significance and how form can influence our appreciation of a painting. By the **composition**, or

BENOZZO GOZZOLI. *Procession of the Magi.* 1459. Medici-Ricardi Palace, Florence, Italy. In contrast to Cézanne, Benozzo Gozzoli considered painting as something ornamental and expressive. He used many details—all richly shown. The painting includes lifelike portraits of members of a family named Medici, who commissioned the painting.

arrangement, an artist uses, he or she takes us into the subject and controls what we are to see. The impact of composition depends largely upon the artist's abilities. The way the artist paints the work will determine how people will interpret and appreciate it.

Painting becomes a new reality—with a language and an internal life of its own.

A viewer must actually *look* at a painting. This may seem to be an unnecessary statement, but it needs to be stressed. Many people can recognize and classify a painting, but often they spend too little time looking at it. To such viewers—even if they are art experts—a copy would be just as good.

The basic knowledge of unchanging factors

JAN VERMEER VAN DELFT. *View of Delft*. 1658-60. The Hague, Mauritshuis, Netherlands.
Landscape painting is not just the imitation of nature, but the creation of a new reality based on nature. Here we are shown not just the city of Delft, but rather the artist's personal view of that city. It is this personal element that attracts us. The painting has an appeal of its own and it has its own reality.

governing the appreciation of a painting have to be learned. This book deals with the traditional techniques of painting, as well as with more recently developed techniques. It also looks at tools and surfaces used by artists, as well as the elements, such as techniques and composition, that make up a painting.

THE ARTIST'S TOOLS

The painter has three basic tools: a palette, a brush, and a palette knife.

Hundreds of years ago, shells or bowls were used to hold paints after they had been mixed. Later, the small wooden **palette**—a thin, oval or rectangular board with a hole for the thumb—was developed.

The **paintbrush** is used to apply paint to the canvas and to provide texture. There is a different brush for each different technique and medium, or material. Normally, round-ended brushes are used for outlining, for blending, and for covering small areas. Short-haired brushes are used to produce thick coats of paint. Long-haired brushes serve to spread the color. Flat brushes are very versatile. Used sideways, they are perfect for outlining. Most brushes are made from bristles and hairs from animals, such as hogs, calves, camels, squirrels, badgers, and sables.

The **palette knife** is very flexible and is usually made of steel. It can be made of bone, ivory, or hard rubber to avoid a chemical reaction that might occur between a steel knife and the paint. The palette knife is mainly used to mix colors and to spread both primer and paint on the surface. It also is sometimes used directly on the surface to create very expressive open forms with paint.

Hands, sponges, and cloths are all used for creating special effects and finishes and for spreading paint.

Artists generally use pencils, pen and ink, charcoal, and chalk for drawing. Great Renaissance painters used silver-pointed styli to work on paper that had already been colored and coated. Then they found

MARINUS REYMERSWAELE. *The Money Changer and his Wife*. 1539. Prado Museum, Madrid, Spain.

Small pictures were often painted on wooden panels during the Romanesque and Gothic periods. **Tempera** paint, generally made of egg yolk, water, and pigments, is applied to a surface and becomes permanent when it dries. During the Renaissance, that drawings made with lead-tipped stilettos were erasable and did not require advance preparation of the paper.

Conté made the first pencil with a mixture of clay and black lead crayon. It is still known today as a Conté crayon. Felt-tipped and ballpoint pens are only occasionally used by artists.

The pen has progressed a long way from the early use of reeds to the metal pen points of today. Among feather pens, goose quills were the most flexible used, but swan, raven, and turkey feathers were also used.

Works of art are also done in crayon, charcoal, pastels, and wax pencil. Today, backgrounds and special effects are sometimes achieved by using an airbrush.

SUPPORTS USED

tempera was used on both wood and canvas. Painting on wooden panels was abandoned in southern Europe during the 17th century. However, in central Europe, artists established a firm tradition of using wooden panels. Careful preparation of the panel allows artists to use delicate, precise brushwork.

People have always felt the urge to express themselves—their feelings, their myths, and their beliefs—as well as to record their possessions, their homes, and the landscape in which they live. The walls of the caves in which prehistoric people lived became surfaces to be decorated with images of all these.

However, throughout the history of art, wood and, later, canvas, have been the most widely used supports for painting. Paintings on wood have been traced to ancient Egypt and Rome. In the Middle Ages, wood became more widely used, especially for religious frontals, polyptychs (hinged panels), and other altar pieces. Canvas gradually became the accepted surface for paintings during the Renaissance, although some artists still used wooden panels occasionally. Panels were made of white poplar, lime, willow, chestnut, cypress, fir, and mahogany woods. Today, fine, laminated three-, four-, or five-ply panels are often used. Some works are painted on canvas that is glued to

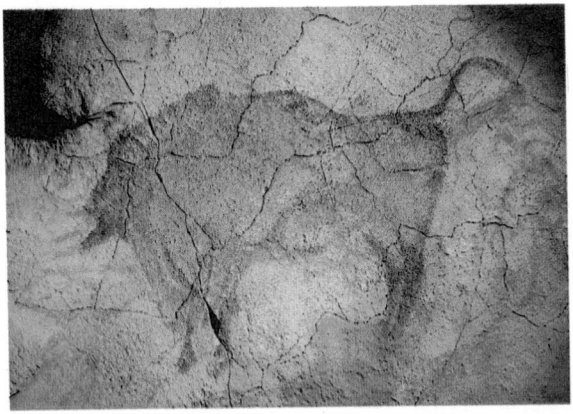

ANONYMOUS. *Large Bison with Straight Tail.* Paleolithic art from the Altamira Caves. Cantabria, Spain.
Cave walls were one of the earliest surfaces on which primitive people drew and painted. The magical character of these paintings does not impair their artistic richness. These artists sought perfection in their art and constantly tried to create beauty.

wood. This practice may combine the best of both techniques.

Today, canvas is the most widely used material, although linen, hemp, cotton, and jute fabrics are also found. For small and medium-sized works, the best material is pure linen. For larger surfaces, hemp is recommended. Canvas has to be primed before being used. For a time, canvases were primed, or coated, with dark colors, but these gradually gave away to white or lighter colors. Other less commonly used materials are silk, velvet, and satin.

The third most common support on which people have painted is walls. Murals from Minoan, Egyptian, and Etruscan art and a few from Greek and Roman art have survived through the years. Mural painting, however, blossomed in the Romanesque period, particularly during the late Gothic era and throughout the Renaissance. During the Baroque period, walls and ceilings were covered with highly decorative images. The artist Goya used oil paint on canvas that was glued to the wall to create his "black" paintings.

Much painting has also been done on copper. Seventeenth-century Flemish art contains good examples of small paintings with careful brushwork.

ÉDOUARD MANET. *Déjeuner sur l'Herbe.* 1863. Musée d'Orsay, Paris.
Only during the Mannerist and Baroque periods did canvas really come into its own in southern European countries. Its light weight and ease of handling made it easy to transport and helped sales. Its lower cost and easy preparation were also important considerations.

ANONYMOUS. *Beatus of Cardeña*. 1200. Art Museum, Gerona, Spain.
Vellum scrolls were frequently used by artists in the early Middle Ages. These were made from sheepskin or calfskin, carefully prepared to get a thin, translucent sheet of material. Scrolls were widely used for writing and illustrating the gospel story, Bibles, and missals from the 4th to the 13th centuries. Since many scrolls have been well preserved over the centuries, we are able to appreciate firsthand much Romanesque art that would have vanished if it had been painted on walls.

ANONYMOUS. *Christ of Saint Clement of Taüll*. 12th century. Museum of Catalan Art, Barcelona, Spain.
Mural painting was at its finest during the Romanesque period. From murals on church walls, uneducated worshippers learned the Christian story. During the Renaissance, Michelangelo created his masterpiece on the ceiling of the Sistine Chapel in the Vatican, but in the Baroque period much of the storytelling part of mural painting vanished.

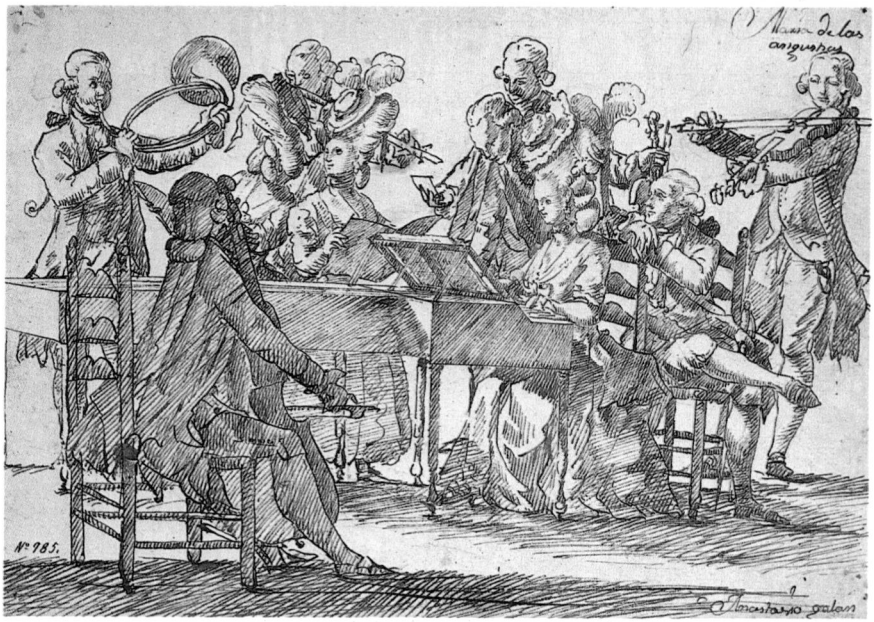

MANUEL TRAMULLES. *The Concert*. Second half of the 17th century. Museum of Modern Art, Barcelona.

Since the 14th century, paper has been a popular surface on which to work out artistic ideas. As it became cheaper, paper allowed artists a freedom to experiment that was not available with other materials. It has been widely used, both for sketching and for finished works, because it is a versatile material that accepts charcoal, pencil, watercolor, and pastel with equal ease. Paper gives a work of art an immediacy and spontaneity not usually found elsewhere.

Zinc and tin have been used in the same way. Slate, marble, and ivory are used, but rarely. Plastics and the human body—either painted or tattooed—are other supports on which people have drawn or painted.

Paper remains the ideal support for drawing. It is especially prized for water-based painting when it is made from linen because of its fine quality and the ease with which brushes, sponges, or palette knives can be used on it. Cotton-based paper, if used for watercolor or gouache, tends to absorb too much water, making the colors less vibrant and clear. Illuminated manuscripts and pictures on scrolls were done by the Greeks and the Romans, and such art flourished in the Middle Ages.

Cardboard, if properly prepared, can also be used as a surface for painting, but it is more often used for drawing and sketching.

Paper is usually white, although indigo and red paper was used during the Renaissance. During the 16th century, blue was the paper color favored by some Italian artists. In the 18th century, some artists worked on gray, off-white, and chamois-colored paper.

TECHNIQUES

FRA ANGELICO. *The Annunciation*. 1430-35. Prado Museum, Madrid. Tempera holds the place of honor in the evolution of painting techniques during the 15th century in Italy. Toward the end of that century, however, tempera began to give way to the first experiments in oils. Unlike oil painting, in which paint can be blended on the surface, tempera does not allow the artist to freely blend pigments on the surface. Rather, each shade must be mixed separately, then applied to its own area on the surface. Cennini said: "Continue like this (using different colors, one after another) making them stand out, then merging them again, delicately blending them."

It is not our intention to explain in great detail all of the techniques used in painting. That alone would take a large and specialized book. Here we will deal with the more widespread techniques and the periods in which they were commonly used. These techniques vary within certain wide divisions. Artists painting in those times had their own techniques, well documented and easy to see today, but jealously guarded as their very own during their working life.

In prehistoric times, people used iron-based pigments (coloring materials) to get red, and manganese-based pigments to get black. Charcoal, and occasionally blood or casein (a product made from sour milk) were used. These were all mixed with animal fat, which brought the pigments together into a primitive "paint."

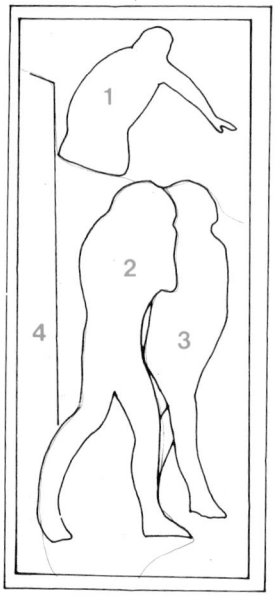

MASACCIO. *The Expulsion from Paradise.* 1424-25. Brancacci Chapel, Santa Maria del Carmine, Florence.
Fresco is the most widely used technique in wall painting. It is based on a very accurate drawing that gives the artist no margin for error. As a rule, it was used for the great Gothic or Renaissance "narrative" paintings and for the "decorative" work of the Baroque and Rococo periods. As in tempera, the fresco technique requires that the artist work on specific areas in sequence. We can see exactly how much of the fresco was done in each work session.

Fresco lends itself to precise line work, rather than smooth and vibrant brushwork. While an artist is influenced by many factors—materials, setting, ideology, and fashion—the technique used has the greatest bearing on his finished work.

ANONYMOUS. *Proculus the Baker and His Wife.* 1st century. San Martino National Museum, Naples, Italy.
Encaustic painting, used in Rome and Egypt, is beautifully demonstrated in this portrait. It is a fine example of the versatility of an artistic technique used in a certain period.

Tempera, fresco, and encaustic painting were techniques used by the ancient Egyptians, Greeks, and Romans. There are many forms of **tempera** that were used for mural painting. In Egypt, the pigments were mixed with water and gums, size (a gluey substance), and both the whites and the yolks of eggs. Then the pigments were applied to the surface separately, with no blending of the colors.

A mixture of egg yolk and the milky sap from the fig tree was used by the great Italian painters of the 14th and 15th centuries. This mixture was sometimes added to frescos to create a mixed, more subtle effect.

A **fresco** is painted onto a base of lime-based plaster using various water-soluble pigments. Mineral-based colors are preferred: St. John's white and slaked lime for whites; natural and burnt ochres for yellows and reds; various earth pigments for reds and greens; lapis lazuli for blue; burnt sienna for browns; and burnt ivory, bone, or coal for blacks. A great deal of advance preparation is required for a fresco. First, a sinopia

ANONYMOUS. *Casa Masferrer Sgraffiti.* Middle of the 18th century. Sant Sadurni d'Osormort.
Sgraffito has been a widely used decorative method for murals from the Renaissance to the present day. The use of a sketch gives the work a drawinglike appearance. The characters look as though they are in negative form. It is used mostly to decorate, but also to explain historical events and to create images. This work shows the symbolic and decorative use of sgraffito.

JAN VAN EYCK. *The Arnolfini Marriage.* 1434. National Gallery, London, England.
The invention of oil paint has been credited, more by tradition than fact, to van Eyck, though it was used by Flemish painters in the 15th century. Italian artist Giorgio Vasari described the advantages of oils this way: "The discovery of oil paints was a most fortunate development for the art of painting. They enhance the brilliance of the colors and require only dedication and loving care. Oil makes the colors softer, sweeter, and more delicate, easier to blend

(an accurate drawing) is made on the plaster. It establishes the outlines and marks out the individual stages of the work. Dry fresco is a process in which pigments are applied to a nearly dry wall, then the painting is finished with color that is mixed with limewater.

The origins of fresco can be found in the ancient cultures of the Near East and the Mediterranean civilizations of Crete, Greece, and Rome. Examples have also been found in China and India. Fresco became an important technique in Byzantium, however. Its importance grew during the Romanesque, Gothic, and Renaissance periods. Early examples of fresco include the Romanesque paintings in the Catalonian Pyrenees. In Italy, Giotto was using the technique in the 14th century, Masaccio in the 15th, and Michelangelo in the 16th. Goya was an outstanding 19th-century master of fresco. In Mexico, Diego Rivera and Orozco used fresco for huge murals.

Some other forms of mural painting look somewhat like fresco, but they never achieve its unique appearance. Oil paints and many of today's modern pigments are now used in wall decoration. Each artist has his or her own technique.

Encaustic painting uses pigments dissolved in melted wax and applied to a surface while hot. Evidence of this type of painting can still be seen on the fronts of

and shade, allowing artists to give their figures a grace, a liveness, and splendor that cause them to appear as if in relief, standing free of the canvas—especially when done with careful design, skill, and good taste."

ANTONI TÀPIES.
***Grafitti*. 1985. Private Collection.**
Modern artists incorporate many of the old methods, but use them to give a modern message. Pictorial art is not only the interaction of form and content. Its techniques, too, have intrinsic value.

some Doric temples. Usually, however, encaustic paintings are on small, specially prepared wooden panels.

Sgraffito is another decorative mural technique. The process is simple. Colored plaster is put on a surface, much like the one used for fresco painting. On top of that, two layers of a thin white plaster are applied. Next, the outlines of the subject are drawn, and then cut through to the undercoat so that a two-color effect is achieved. Often put on building fronts, sgraffito dates back to Renaissance times. It was used in the 18th century and is still used today as a decorative feature on neoclassical buildings.

Oil painting is by far the best-known technique, and is used on wood panels or on canvas. Pigments are ground and mixed with oil, usually linseed or walnut oil. Although Jan van Eyck is credited for its "invention," he did not really invent it, for the technique was well known from ancient times. Van Eyck and other 15th-century Flemish painters, however, used oils enthusiastically. Oil painting has many advantages—particularly the brilliance of its colors and the ability it gives artists to make changes by superimposing brush strokes. With oils, artists have much greater freedom of action. But any corrections made with oils do become visible with the passage of time. From the 16th century on, oil painting has become more and more popular. It has been modified to meet the needs of different artists and styles of painting.

Contrast the almost flat colors of van Eyck with the more rounded figures of Rubens. Van Eyck removed fatty substances from the oil in which he mixed his pigments. Rubens used a thickened oil to which he had added turpentine and a soft resin varnish, sometimes even a beeswax. Today, most painters use prepared oil paint that is sold in tubes, which became widely available in the 1860s.

Another technique uses **acrylic paints**, which are water-based, very flexible, and dry quickly (unlike oils). Also unlike oil paints, acrylics are highly resistant to atmospheric contamination.

In **collage**, various materials—photographs, newspaper cuttings, even solid objects—are used to form a composition, which is sometimes affixed to an oil or acrylic base. **Kineticism** tries to reproduce movement in a composition. It introduces additional elements

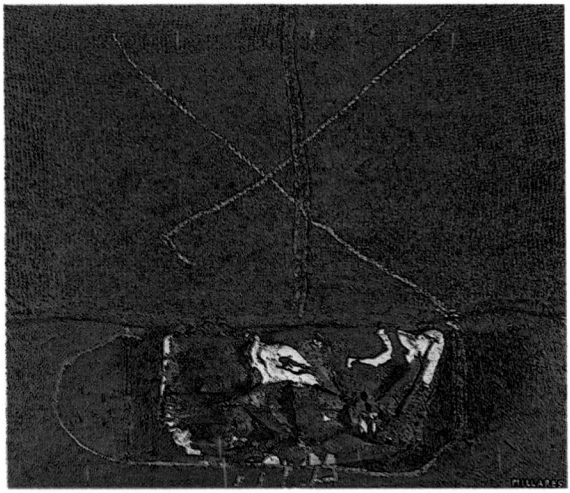

MANUEL MILLARES. *Manikin*. 1962. Private Collection.
Millares achieves the textures and tensions of composition with his collage of torn sackcloth. The impact of his work is enhanced by his use of white, black, and some red. He shuns classical brushwork and seeks communication through broken, complex forms. His work expresses his deep despair. His forms are a coarse imitation of reality. Reality does not exist for Millares—all that exists is a sense of dehumanization.

LUIS PARET Y ALCÁZAR. *The Go-Between and the Lovers*. 1784. Private Collection.
Watercolor painting has many possibilities but, as with pastel painting, it demands that the artist have great technical skill and a vast knowledge of the medium used. Its rediscovery in the 18th century put it at the same level as the more traditional media. Watercolor painting is a technique that has enjoyed varying popularity. It is not used often by well-known artists, but is used mostly by so-called watercolorists, who are true specialists in their art. Watercolorists today tend to use the white base (surface) as an essential part of the painting's composition.

and technical objects. It also uses tricks of perspective and optical illusion.

One well-known decorative technique uses lacquer. Originally from China, **lacquering** was introduced to Europe in the 17th century. It became more extensively used in the 18th century for furniture decoration. Lacquer is a hard, shiny varnish made from the sap found in certain trees.

There is continuous interaction between painting and drawing. Generally speaking, a drawing is the first stage of a work of art—a sketch, a plan, or an outline of a proposed painting, called a cartoon—and has always been executed with relative speed. From the 18th century on, however, drawing was regarded as an artistic achievement in its own right. Talent for drawing has always been recognized in China and Japan, where the term *hua* denotes painting, drawing,

MAURICE QUENTIN DE LA TOUR. *Portrait of Madame Pompadour*. The Louvre, Paris.
By the 18th century, pastel had become established as an art form in its own right, especially in France. Maurice Quentin de la Tour was admitted to the French Royal Academy because of a series of pastel portraits he submitted. A certain artificial air, in keeping with the elaborate fashions of 18th century literature, characterizes his work. Pastel is versatile and well suited to more spontaneous and less carefully drawn creations. Here, however, we see what can be achieved with pastel by a skilled artist with a thorough knowledge of the technique.

and calligraphy as artistic elements of equal merit and value.

Works on paper have different names according to the technique used. The most common techniques are pencil, charcoal, and red chalk (known as sanguine). There also are pastel, wax, watercolor, and gouache.

Pastel is a dry technique. The pigments are ground, mixed with an adhesive, and formed into small sticks. Its best feature is the velvety texture that it leaves. But it is easily smudged and can be affected by sunlight and humidity. Pastel was widely used in the 18th century, particularly by artists in France. More recently, pastel has been used by Degas and Picasso.

Wax is greasier than pastel. Pigments are dissolved in wax and other meltable substances, then are made into small sticks similar to those of pastel. Wax colors are vivid and adhere well to paper.

ANONYMOUS. *Baptism of Christ*. 6th century. Ariani Baptistery, Ravenna, Italy.
Mosaic is one of the most widely appreciated artistic techniques. Figures and decorative drawing are done in the artistic styles of the period in which the mosaics were designed. Sometimes mosaics reproduce actual paintings. For example, the mosaics in the basilica of Saint Peter's, Rome, faithfully copy the original of Poussin's *Martyrdom of Saint Erasmus*. The Near East, Rome, and, above all, Byzantium have left us many fine examples of mosaic work. Because it is durable, mosaic gives us some idea of paintings done at the same time—paintings that have long since disappeared.

Watercolor painting uses pigments that are held together by gum arabic and thinned with water. The effect of light is achieved by the tone of the background, without the use of any white pigment. Therefore the support of a watercolor painting is very important to its artistic effect.

Gouache differs from watercolor in that white pigment is added to the colored pigments. The addition of white gives the paint an opaque effect that is not seen in watercolor painting. Gouache was first used in the illuminated pages of medieval manuscripts and was most widely used in France and England in the 18th and 19th centuries.

No overview of techniques would be complete without mentioning gilding, enameling, stained glass, and mosaic. **Gilding**—the application of gold leaf or gold powder to a surface—was used as a background on some paintings of the Gothic and pre-Renaissance periods. The skill, however, goes back much further, to ancient China, India, and Persia, as well as Egypt, Greece, and Rome. The high price of gold has prevented it from being widely used today. Imitation gilding, using paint, is pointless, for the paint soon tarnishes.

There are many forms of **enameling**. The term generally describes a glassy coating fused to porcelain or metal. Enameling was most popular during the Gothic period and is still widely practiced today. In the 18th century, enameling was used to decorate jewelry, clocks, snuffboxes, and the like.

Stained glass and mosaics, like the enameling and decoration of ceramics, are based on the use of firing techniques. They are included here because the composition, design, and decoration are often the work of painters.

These then are the most commonly used media and techniques. They have influenced the work of those artists who have used and developed them. Artists choose their media and techniques carefully in order to enhance the artistic message they want to convey.

THE ELEMENTS OF FORM

When we look at any picture, the first things we see are images with distinct shapes. They may be realistic or they may be abstract. We try to recognize elements within the picture and then to evaluate them. This is when we may confuse physical reality with artistic reality. Abstract art emphasizes pure form and has encouraged people to appreciate form for its own sake. Some shapes are best suited to drawing, or linear depiction, and some to a brush technique.

An emphasis on line, or linear technique, has normally been used in, and been associated with, highly intellectual types of art. In those types of art, artists base their work on ideas rather than on trying to affect the viewer's senses. It is, therefore, not surprising to find works where the line is the basic element binding the separate parts together into geometric shapes.

FERDINAND LEGÉR. *Homage to Jacques-Louis David.* 1948-49. Museum of Modern Art, Paris. This line drawing clearly illustrates the feeling of the work. It suggests a concise, clear, sharp, and strong structure. It encloses each of the elements, leaving them individual and a part of the whole at the same time. The artist uses the line instead of the spontaneous brush stroke.

FRANS HALS. *Gypsy Girl.* 1628-30. The Louvre, Paris.
The Dutch painter Frans Hals shows the value of loose brushwork. His paintings communicate to the viewer through their spontaneity and are vital, dynamic, and expressive. In this way, he shows a clear relationship between content and artistic language. On the other hand, open or **pictorial form** occurs when the artist expresses himself or herself with a much freer form. An example of an abstract artist who uses this form is Jackson Pollock, who relies on sensual appeal.

This is characteristic of Renaissance, Neo-Classicism, Cubist, and Rationalist paintings.

Shapes can be decorative or speculative. Decorative shapes add many elements to the formal structure of a composition. These elements contribute to any work of art. A picture of a king will have a lot of ornamental elements suitable for a king. These elements may be overemphasized or reduced to a minimum.

Throughout history, artists have created works in which shapes themselves have become the real subjects of the pictures. What is interesting in these works is not the theme, but the shapes making up that theme.

We have talked about tools, supports, and techniques, without talking about elements. The genius of the artist, Velázquez, for example, is that he can

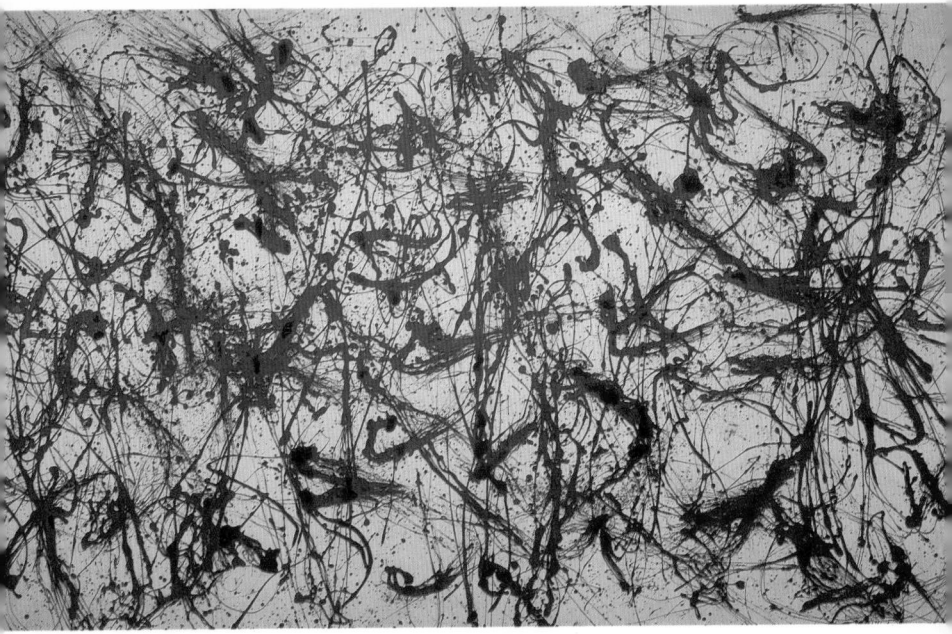

JACKSON POLLOCK. *No.* 32. 1950. Kunstsammlung Nordrhein Westfalen, Dusseldorf, West Germany.
In this work, line takes on an expressive value but is used in a completely new way. Paint has been dripped or smeared onto a canvas lying on the ground. The artist worked from all sides, calling it **action painting**. Pollock's treatment of space is quite new. The viewer is aware of both the surface of the work, and of drips of paint that seem to float in space behind the surface. The picture has no traditional perspective.

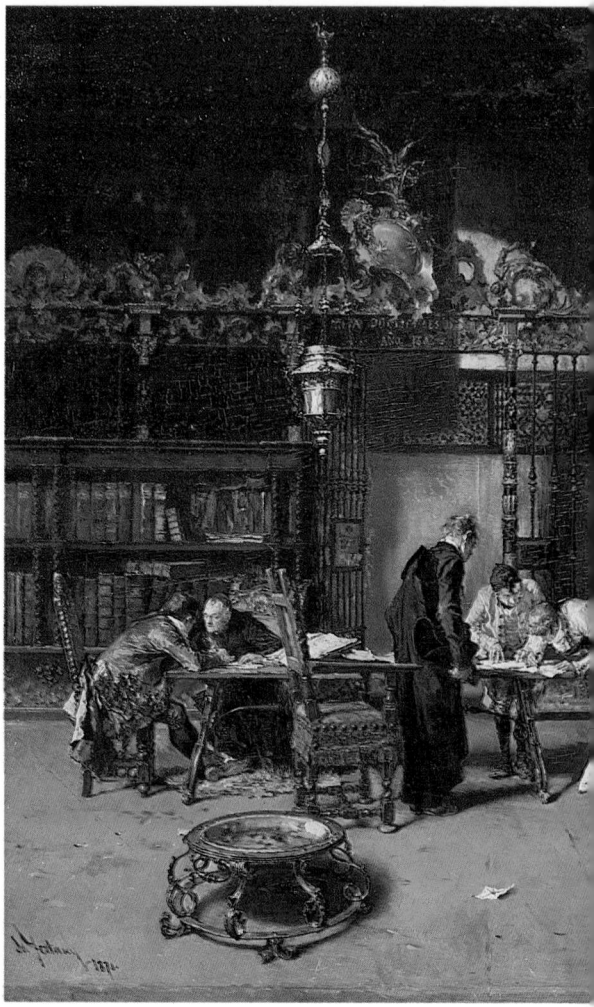

MARIANO FORTUNY. *The Spanish Wedding.* 1870. Museum of Modern Art, Barcelona.
The freedom that artists used throughout the 19th century is best illustrated in the work of painters such as Meissonier of France and Fortuny. The frivolous style is appropriate to its subject matter. It is far from a sturdy realism.

combine the essential with what might be called added detail.

All works of art can be reduced to geometrical shapes. The structure of these shapes is basic and the painter forgets it at his or her own risk. The circle, the square, the triangle, the rhomboid, the prism, and the cube are all shapes in the elements of a picture. Some painters emphasize them; others hide them beneath lots of details. Artists also use straight and curved lines. The straight line gives a feeling of stability when used

vertically or horizontally. A diagonal line gives energy to a subject. A curve is always dynamic, except when it forms a circle. Then it conveys great stability. The straight line expresses security; the curve usually expresses instability.

The proportion, or balance, between the various elements is important. When it is applied to the human figure, this proportion is called a canon, or general principle. The head is most frequently the basic unit for human proportion. In ancient Egyptian art, there

PETER PAUL RUBENS. *The Three Graces.* 1636-38. Prado Museum, Madrid.
An ideal of beauty runs through the works of many great artists. In *The Three Graces*, women are symbols of physical beauty and also examples of the changing taste of each age. The rounded beauties of Rubens contrast with the slim figures of the Italian painter Botticelli. Both artists, however, reflect the style and the ideas of their age.

are paintings that seem to use the middle finger as a basic unit of measurement.

The Renaissance theorist Alberti established that the ideal height of a person should be equal to 7½ times the height of his or her head. Alberti based this ratio on studies of real human beings. Dürer experimented with figures having a height ratio of 7, 8, 9, and 10 heads. The Mannerists distorted the classical rule to, in extreme cases, ratios of 1:11 or even 1:12.

EDVARD MUNCH. *The Scream*. 1893. National Gallery, Oslo, Norway. The curved line is the link in all so-called Expressionist art. Munch, by means of a curved line, defines perfectly an agitated and anguished state of mind. The feeling of emotional instability is shown by the distortion of the figures and shapes. The shape itself is full of expressive meaning. In Munch's work, it is hard to distinguish between form and content, because his method is the meaning.

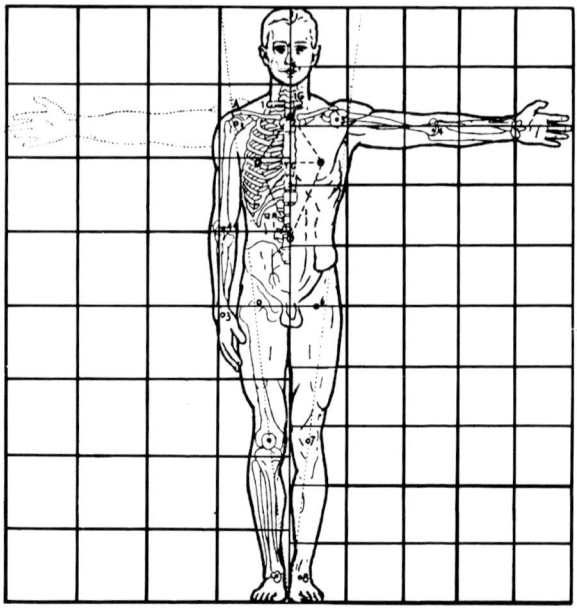

Proportions of the Human Body

PARMIGIANINO. *The Madonna with the Long Neck*. 1531. Uffizi Gallery, Florence.
The golden rule of proportion has changed throughout the history of art. A ratio of 1:8—total body height equals the height of eight heads—was most widely used as a classical norm, although this was modified in the 16th century. Any change from the rule has great significance. Elongation, or lengthening, of the human figure gives it a certain majesty, but also a feeling of insecurity.

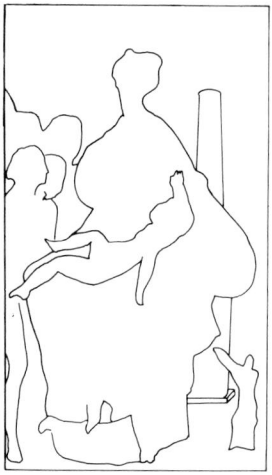

Ideals of beauty are not expressed only by the general rule, but take many forms. In *The Three Graces*, in which women represent physical and spiritual beauty, the painter expresses his aesthetic taste, or sense of beauty. For example, the figures in the works of Botticelli, Raphael, and Rubens have come to represent the aesthetic norm of the 14th, 15th and 16th centuries.

Saint Augustine said, "All that exists must have form." We would add that the basic element in a picture is shape, whether it is representational (realistic) or abstract.

THE STRUCTURE OF A WORK

ANONYMOUS. *Nativity*. 13th century. Side altar in Sagas, Solsona. Diocesan Museum.
An early type of perspective, or viewpoint, allowed the main element to dominate the upper half of a composition. Each figure has its planned place in a work, and the way in which figures are placed determines their relative importance in the whole. Having the figures look in many directions creates a liveliness in an imaginary space.

Shapes acquire a meaning in space. This meaning gives structure to a composition. Artists must arrange all of their elements so that they fulfill their function in the picture. It is this arrangement of shapes that determines the value of a work of art.

Artistic language is complex and is always changing, but it obeys a certain logic. If that logic is not followed, the viewer will not respond.

RAPHAEL. *The School of Athens*. 1512. Stanza della Segnatura, Vatican Palace, Rome, Italy.
The School of Athens is one of the best examples of the logical arrangement of objects in space as they would appear in reality. The artificial, or scientific, perspective with its converging lines arranges the composition so that the different elements take on their correct dimensions in the picture. The **central vanishing point**—the focus of all the lines of perspective—orders the whole layout. The architectural features follow these lines, allowing the eye to appreciate the composition. This is the application of the Renaissance definition of perspective: each element is of a size corresponding to the position it occupies.

Painters must know the rules, absorb them, and forget them. Only then can they develop their own individual languages—their styles—which will distinguish them from other artists. Throughout the history of art, tastes have changed and aesthetic conflicts have been frequent. The art of each movement has to be analyzed separately. For example, Gothic art must be evaluated differently than Romantic art.

One of the main aspects of the composition of a painting is the distribution of the elements in space so that the viewer is completely satisfied. In much of the art of Western cultures since the Renaissance, the viewer looks at a work as if through a window (the picture frame) and does not see an exact representation of reality, but rather a new reality—artistic reality.

Perspective allows us to position objects in space by following our intuition or experience. Artistic perspective has developed in many ways and has been influenced by philosophy, religion, and society.

For primitive artists, space was god-given, and they did not impose their own ideas onto it. Foreground and background were defined according to the

ALEJO FERNÁNDEZ. *The Virgin of the Navigators*. 1530s. Reales Alcazares, Seville, Spain.
What has been called hierarchical or theological perspective emphasizes the most important figures. We see the Virgin welcoming into her protection the members of the Navigators' Guild (one of them is supposed to be Christopher Columbus) who appear small in comparison with the main figure. This proportion, emphasizing the

positioning of figures. Subjects were put on the surface without any particular order, though at times, diagonally placed figures created a sort of accidental perspective. The Romans positioned their figures in a more ordered fashion. Each figure was to go in its own place according to a plan. Horizontal or vertical side-by-side position made up the composition, and the main figure occupied the upper part of the picture. Religious influence is clearly present in this style. Space is arranged to express the idea that a distance exists between humans and the divine. The Gothic period introduced the idea of theological perspective. God the Father, Christ, and the Virgin Mary are represented as larger than saints and angels, with human beings shown as the smallest of all.

This medieval hierarchy, or order, was abandoned during the Renaissance. Humans became the center

central figure, replaces reality with an idea and is used for narrative effect.

ANONYMOUS. *Oxen trampling grain.* Valley of the Kings. Tomb of Menna, Thebes, Egypt. This uses an almost child-like perspective if we judge by reality. The worker is not on top of a mountain of wheat, but in the middle of a wheat field. With this interpretation, the presence of the oxen, placed diagonally and in the foreground, is easier to understand. The painting is the graphic representation of a moment. Although it sometimes comes near to visual reality, the painting never duplicates it. Artistic reality has many forms, which is one reason it makes it such an interesting subject for study.

DIEGO VELÁZQUEZ. *The Maids of Honor (Las Meninas).* 1656. Prado Museum, Madrid.

PABLO PICASSO. *The Maids of Honor (Las Meninas).* 1957. Picasso Museum, Barcelona.

Velázquez's ideas on artistic reality are very clearly expressed in this picture. He uses traditional perspective, to which he has added an imaginative perspective. Thus he creates new or artistic space in which the elements of the picture do not appear to match physical reality. There are many questions: What exactly is the artist painting? Where are the king and queen? What role does the princess play in her group of attendants? Velázquez has brought together a number of people and elements and implied others. Here we have one of the most imaginative works in the history of art. Its great merit is that we can enjoy it without understanding all its subtleties. This was the reason Picasso reinterpreted the painting in the best way he knew—with pictorial shapes.

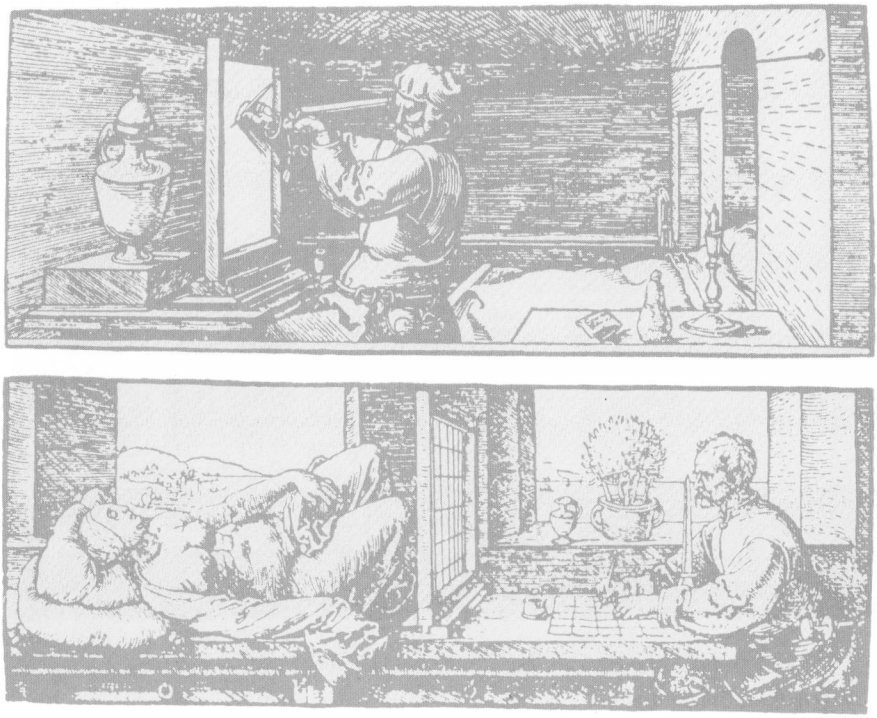

ALBRECHT DÜRER. *Tools to Duplicate Perspective.* 1525. Mechanical and mathematical means were used and described by Dürer. The *fixed viewfinder* allowed the artist to observe the subject through a lens, to trace its outline, and to transfer it to paper by means of a grid, which divided the image into a number of squares. The other system illustrated is the *viewfinder*. It allowed the artist to see his subject through a lens placed between him and it.

and the measure of all things. There was no longer any need to show the difference between the earthly and the spiritual. Space was distributed according to the human figures shown. Artists created perspective in which they sized people and objects in relation to their position within the picture.

We can see the development of perspective in the 14th century. Artists created three-dimensional space while representing reality, although there was no formal perspective. In the 15th century, artists' status grew with the invention and use of scientific perspective.

CANALETTO. *View of the Church of the Salute and Entrance to the Grand Canal, Venice*. 1730. The Louvre, Paris.

The *camera obscura* was a basic tool of the **veduta painters**—painters of places, usually towns. True depiction of a landscape takes for granted the use of some optical device to prevent any error. The **camera obscura** is a small, portable box with a circular hole in the top. In the box is a lens carrier. The lens can be moved up or down in the carrier, changing the distance between the lens and the flat base of the box, where the paper is placed. On the lens carrier, a

Painting changed from being the work of a craftsperson to the work of an artist. **Pictorial space**, in which any point could be taken as the center, was created. Usually a central perspective view was presented, in which the horizon coincided with the vanishing point.

Many theories were developed during the Renaissance to explain techniques of perspective. In central Europe, practical and theoretical studies did not appear until the 16th century, although similar solutions had been found by painters in the previous century.

Jan van Eyck, using a mirror, obtained curved perspectives, as he showed in *The Arnolfini Marriage*. Roger van der Weiden, although he did not use a scientific perspective system, obtained lifelike results.

By the end of the 15th century and the beginning of the 16th century, the theories and practice of perspective had been developed. New ways to organize space had been widely exchanged among artists. **Color perspective** appeared—suggesting a movement into space with the use of lighter tones toward the back of a picture. Color perspective was used alone or with linear perspective. Venetian painters favored a color

movable, inclined mirror captures the image and projects it onto the paper, where it is traced by the painter. This direct process has now been replaced by slides that the artist projects directly onto canvas. The painter chooses the landscape. Then, by using light and color, he or she introduces atmospheric factors that the camera obscura cannot capture.

system, and the Florentines used the single vanishing point as their means of organizing space. Leonardo da Vinci, working in Florence, wrote: "The science of painting includes all the colors of the base and the forms of the bodies that take on these colors, together with their proportions, according to whether they are near to or far away. This is the mother of perspective, by which I mean the science of the lines of vision, a science that may be divided into three parts: the first includes the linear construction of the bodies [linear perspective], the second, the change in color in relation to distance [perspective of color], and the third, the

ANDREA POZZO. *False Cupola*. 1685. Church of San Ignatius, Rome.
In the works of the Jesuit painter Andrea Pozzo, visual trickery comes very close to the illusions found in Baroque art. This illusion of a cupola should be viewed from the entrance to the church. Pozzo does not support the idea of multiple vanishing points. His vanishing point is both geometrical and symbolic. Pozzo wrote that "the task of the painter is to draw all the lines . . . to the real focus point, that of Divine glory."

ANONYMOUS. *Christ and the Apostles*. End of the 12th century. Diocese of Urgel. Museum of Catalan Art, Barcelona. Seeking harmony of composition, the artist has arranged his elements to the right and the left of a central axis. He applies the rule of perfection in which two of the fundamental points are harmony and symmetry. The figure of Christ occupies the center. The apostles, in two groups of six, face inward on either side. In theory, if we were to fold the picture down its central axis, the group on the right would exactly match the figures on the left.

loss of sharpness of the image, also in relation to distance [diminishing perspective]."

In this period of transition between the order of the 15th century and the disorder of the 16th, artists began using a **perspective of illusion**, in which optical tricks make us see things that do not really exist.

Creating the illusion of spaces involves the use of multiple vanishing points. Mantegna introduces us to multiple vanishing points with his decoration of the *Nuptial Bed* in the Ducal Palace at Mantua. He uses greatly foreshortened figures to suggest a deep field of view.

Venetian painters, in composing their great works, used several vanishing points arranged around a central axis, or imaginary line. At times, the vanishing points were outside the painting, which created the effect of great energy. Because painters want to make their compositions believable, they must sometimes change the strict rules of perspective. For example, the Mannerists knew the rules, but broke them because of the needs of their particular art and, thus, produced some surprising results.

TINTORETTO. *The Washing of the Feet*. 1547. Prado Museum, Madrid. Mannerism broke with the traditional symmetrical axis, which coincided with a central vanishing point. Tintoretto foreshortened diagonal perspective and fanned out his figures, widening the field of vision. Here we see a composition with a deep field of view. It is created by background architectural features and delicate areas of light and shade.

In the 17th century, many artists questioned the values that, at the time, formed the basis of all scientific thought. German astronomer Johannes Kepler's theory was that parallel lines meet in the infinite. The infinite appeared as illusory space. It is not surprising, then, that rules began to evolve for illusion, although it had been in common use since the end of the 15th century. Baroque art of the 17th century, however, sought the infinite, the undefined. Decoration of walls, vaults,

PERUGINO. *The Delivery of the Keys*. 1480-82. Sistine Chapel, Rome. Even at the height of the Renaissance, Perugino continued to follow the idea that the center is the most important spot in a composition. He arranged his groups around a theological center—in this case the key, symbol of the Papacy. The key, placed on the axis of symmetry, is the point around which the whole painting revolves. Groups, rather than the individual, predominate.

FRANCISCO ZURBARÁN. *Still Life*. 1633. Prado Museum, Madrid.
The artist emphasized the individual, rather than the group. The composition singles out the objects, placing them side by side, rather than one in front of another. The painting can be divided into separate parts, each of which has its own value and interest. It is unlike those compositions in which individual elements are important only because of their association with others.

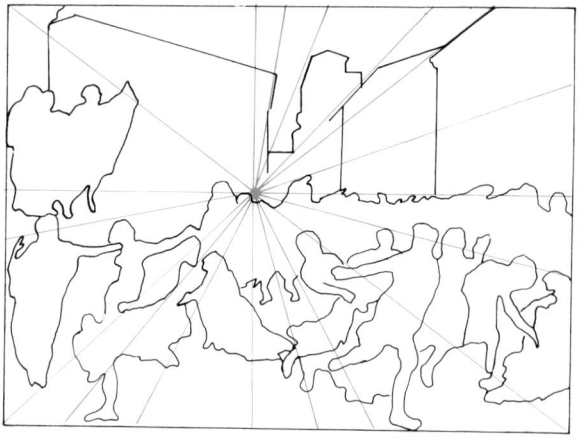

NICOLAS POUSSIN. *The Rape of the Sabines*. 1637-38. The Louvre, Paris.
This is an outstanding example of centralized composition. Poussin creates a deep, open space, and places his figures within lines radiating out from the center of the picture toward infinity. This type of open composition gives a dynamic quality to the whole. It creates a series of emotional tensions. In this way, the meaning and the dramatic effect of the work come from the combination of visual style and formal composition.

and ceilings tried to create integral space. Columns were severely foreshortened and designs were made so figures could be painted on curved surfaces, such as domed ceilings, and still appear lifelike when viewed from a proper position.

In easel painting, **aerial perspective**—a subtle combination of color and shade—is used. The elements of a picture are defined in space by the use of light and color.

The 17th-century style of Baroque continued into the 18th with the introduction, in Venice, of veduta.

ANTOINE WATTEAU. *Gilles*. 1717-19. The Louvre, Paris.
The artist shows his subjects in different ways, with the viewer in mind. The line of the horizon is used to give meaning to the work. A low horizon gives the figure greater prominence. Watteau uses a clown, rather than a king or saint, as his main character. He gives this traditional figure of fun a grandeur.

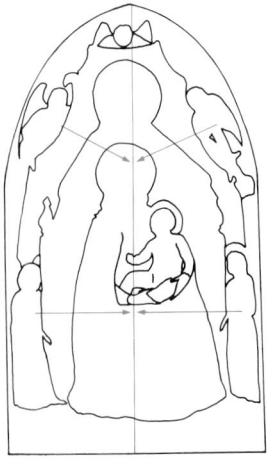

MASACCIO/MASOLINO. *The Virgin and Child with Saint Anne*. 1424. Uffizi Gallery, Florence.
Enclosed compositions are based on a central line or axis. All elements group around this theoretical central area in which the main figure is placed. In this picture, medieval symmetry is used with a theological center. A certain "humanizing" of the figures gives the work a modern feeling.

Veduta is a style that brought science and nature closer together. Algorotti wrote: "Painters will have to use the optical camera in the same way that astronomers use the telescope and physicists the microscope. All these instruments lead to a better understanding of nature." The camera obscura reproduced perspective in the same way as a modern photographic camera.

Painters today still use traditional techniques of perspective. **Flat perspective**, in which the elements of a picture are juxtaposed (placed side by side), is also commonly used. It is linked to the use of different viewpoints (in Cubism) or of color (in Impressionism).

PETER PAUL RUBENS. *Rustic Dance*. 1630. Prado Museum, Madrid. In painting, the *dynamics of space* almost always means the blending of the various parts into a whole. The use of the curved line and the open, fluid brush technique help tie the composition into a whole. They are complementary elements, used individually. In this work, Rubens seeks an overall, rather than a particular, effect.

The New Realists, using camera and transparencies, promoted what is called photographic perspective.

Composition in painting emphasizes the blending of elements into a whole. The idea of symmetry, or balance, is important. Early painters established a symmetrical axis and placed elements in an orderly way to the left and the right of this axis. Romantic and Gothic artists stressed this organization and repeated elements in an identical manner. Renaissance artists, however, tended to balance space with groups of figures. Renaissance technique, then, resulted in

EDGAR DEGAS. *La Toilette*. 1896. Musée d'Orsay, Paris.
In some of his work, Degas treated his subjects as simply elements of the composition. He pursued visions of reality that are closer to photography than to painting. His abrupt viewpoints were novel. They tended to lessen the importance of the subject.

greater individuality for both figures and objects, all of which then had their own personalities.

Mannerist artists organized space in an irregular way. At first look, Mannerist space might appear disorganized, but it is never unbalanced. It is a kind of symmetrical asymmetry. Although it shows itself in different ways, balance is critical to all painting.

Symmetry is closely linked to different types of compositions. **Enclosed composition** is normally based on a central line or axis—all elements are associated with the theoretical center of the picture. It is typical of the medieval and Renaissance works.

JUAN VAN DER HAMEN. *Still Life*. The National Gallery of Art, Washington, D.C., U.S.A.
The use of a high horizon seems to put all the elements on display individually. With a raised horizon line, the forms in the picture appear to lean toward the viewer, as they would if set out on a market stall. Thus, the viewer dominates the scene.

PERUGINO. *Virgin and Child with Four Saints.* 1479. Vatican Museum, Rome.
This work clearly shows the importance of the horizon. It is at midheight in relation to the four saints, but it is low for the Virgin Mary on her throne. The saints are set at the same level as the viewer, with the Virgin higher and thus more important. This technique adds force to the work.

An **open composition** may have elements arranged around a central or a lateral (side) axis, or with an external vanishing point. It is a composition in which the elements appear out of place, off center, and sometimes even left out of the painting. This was particularly done by Mannerist and Baroque artists. As a general rule, enclosed compositions unite elements; open compositions break apart elements.

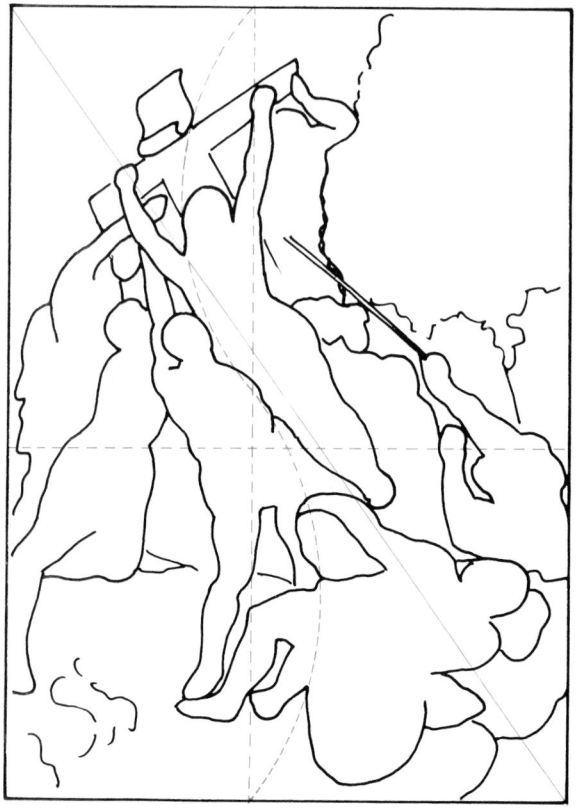

PETER PAUL RUBENS. *The Raising of the Cross.* 1609-10. Antwerp Cathedral, Antwerp, Belgium.
This is a complex work. To obtain a dynamic space, the artist used both a diagonal line and a curved S-pattern. The result is a scene of great tension, matching the event portrayed.

LUCA SIGNORELLI. *Holy Family*. 1480. Uffizi Gallery, Florence.
Here the circle dictates the composition of the whole work, which is made to fit into the framework. The artist set up a gentle rhythm. He linked the bowed posture of Joseph with that of the Virgin Mary. The picture has a significant theoretical center point: the Christ Child.

A composition may be unified or nonunified. In a unified picture, elements interact and are superimposed on each other. In a nonunified picture, elements are juxtaposed and individualized.

In a unified work, the artists emphasize the whole composition. They do not emphasize one part at the expense of the whole. This is typical of Baroque works. Nonunified composition deals with objects and figures more separately. In the Realist works, figures and objects are essential elements in composition. Unified and nonunified composition can provide either great clarity or great obscurity. Individual objects are easier to understand than a general overall effect, but the fewer individual elements or details a picture has, the easier it is to understand.

A very important aspect of composition in perspective is the location of the horizon. Elements are not placed in relation to the horizon merely to please the eye, but to add emphasis to the content of the work. Anything placed on or above the horizon becomes more important and tends to dominate the work. Objects below the line of the horizon appear smaller and become less important. A high horizon reduces the importance of the subject; a low horizon increases it.

Elements in a painting may be based on the circle, the oval, the triangle, the square, or even the pentagon or the hexagon. Sometimes these shapes are used

RUDOLF VON ES. *Nativity*. 1370. Library, Munich, West Germany. The golden section, or divine proportion, was widely used during the Renaissance. Within a rectangle, divided into two equal parts, a new space is created based on the arc of a circle with its center on the midpoint of the longest side. The artist has placed the reclining Virgin within the arc, helping us to visualise the layout.

PETER PAUL RUBENS. *Hélène Fourment and Her Children*. 1636-37. The Louvre, Paris.

Rubens's work follows a preestablished plan in which geometry orders the whole. The center of this composition is a circle, with the S-shaped lines linking the other elements smoothly to the principal figures. Baroque freedom was still restricted by geometry, though the curves that predominate here adapt to the gentleness of the whole work.

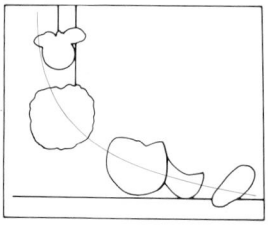

JUAN SÁNCHEZ COTÁN. *Still Life*. 1603. Fine Arts Gallery, San Diego, U.S.A. This plastic, speculative layout is one of Cotán's most frequently used devices. Structural strength is established by arranging the objects along the arc of a circle. Here the painter emphasized the laws of geometry, which became more important than the real appearance of the objects themselves.

EDGAR DEGAS. *Glass of Absinthe*. 1876. Musée d'Orsay, Paris.
Degas is a master in the use of space. This could almost be a photographic approach –the people pushed to the right-hand edge of the composition–but the pictorial value and the zigzag construction confirm the superiority of painting over the mere objectivity of the camera. Degas uses the eye of the photographer but introduces the subjective view of the artist. This is no instant snapshot of the two people. Degas studied them, took in the whole scene, and only then gave us his own interpretation of it. This is the painting's greatest value–it captures an atmosphere, rather than a moment.

individually, sometimes together. To give feeling to a composition, figures are arranged in straight lines—vertical, horizontal, or diagonal—or in curves.

Regular geometrical shapes give a feeling of order. Irregular forms give a feeling of energy and action.

A work of art is not merely the product of form and shape, but of various complementary methods of facilitating interpretation. A circle tends to focus the action; curved or diagonal lines give dynamism. A wide-based triangle shows stability; an inverted triangle shows instability. Geometry forms the basis of pictorial

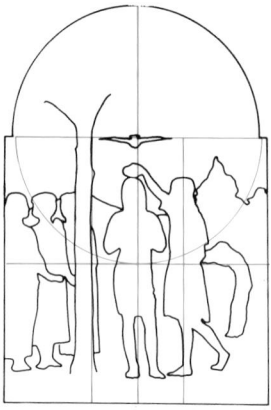

PIERO DELLA FRANCESCA. *The Baptism of Christ*. 1448-50. National Gallery, London.

PIERO DELLA FRANCESCA. *Brera Altarpiece*. 1472-76. Brera Art Gallery, Milan, Italy.

In *Baptism of Christ*, Piero della Francesca used geometry to regulate the space. It is divided into three equal parts vertically and two horizontally. Symmetry demands that the tree trunk be placed to the left of center, balancing the figure of John the Baptist on the right. The Holy Spirit occupies a position two-thirds up from the base. It is the center of a circle that takes in the top two-thirds of the picture, and its size is linked to that of John the Baptist's arm. In *Altarpiece of Brera*, the circle dominates the composition, based on a symmetrical axis, and gives it dynamism.

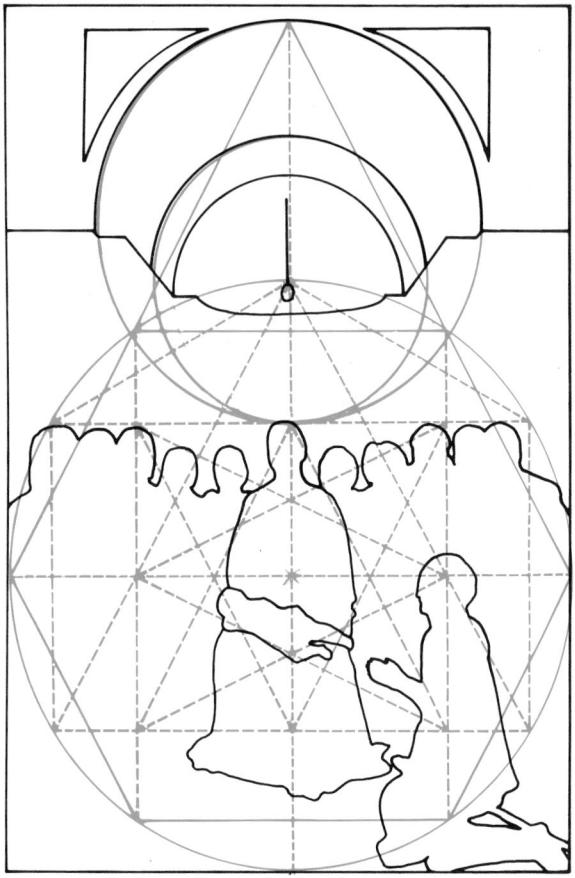

art. A viewer's appreciation of this fact depends upon the number of added details—details that are added both to complement and obstruct the geometrical structure of a work.

A picture, however, is not just drawing and geometry. It has the two essential elements of color and tone.

Colors can be cold (blues and violets) or warm (reds and oranges). Different terms have been used for this double aspect: positive and negative; active and passive. Artists use color to attract or distance the viewer.

Cold colors are used intellectually. Warm colors, on the other hand, allow the viewer to involve his or her feelings. Mannerist artists used cold colors, while Renaissance artists used warm colors. Color alone, however, does not determine a viewer's response to the painting.

EL GRECO. *Laocoön.* 1610-14. The National Gallery of Art, Washington, D.C.
The Mannerism of El Greco broke with the warm, glowing colors of the Renaissance by using distant, cold tones. The work is frozen and intellectual, distancing itself from our senses. Both the unreality of proportion and the attitudes of the figures emphasize this distancing.

VINCENT VAN GOGH. *Self Portrait with Hat.* 1887. Stedelijk Museum, Amsterdam, Netherlands.
Van Gogh used complimentary colors and broken color, techniques of the Impressionists, to achieve vibrant visual effects. The Impressionists sought to record their perceptual experiences—to paint what they saw. The startling luminous color in Van Gogh's paintings suggests that he was recording more than simply visual truth. His heightened contrasts of complimentary colors and his fierce brush strokes seem to express a turbulent emotional state. Van Gogh, like the Impressionists, strove to record what he saw, but he also left us a record of another kind of truth—the emotions of the artist.

JEAN-FRANÇOIS MILLET. *El Angelus.* 1858-59. Musée d'Orsay, Paris.
A quiet grandeur pervades Millet's *El Angelus*. It expresses a sense of unity, a sense that the man and woman are one with the land and the sky. This effect is achieved, in great part, by Millet's orchestration of the tone relationships in the painting. Millet makes the tone move from dark to light in subtle gradations. The rhythm set up by this gradual movement can be associated with the dignified rhythms of processional ceremonies—an association quite unlike what one might expect from the humble subject matter. Compare Millet's painting with the Caravaggio on page 54. Caravaggio made his dark areas and light areas contrast sharply rather than allowing them to merge with one another, as Millet did. Caravaggio used this high contrast to create visual excitement, an excitement that helps to convey the drama of the subject: the moment of the conversion of Saint Paul on the road to Damascus.

Painters use a harmony of tones that brings a unity of color to their work. Paintings that contain complementary colors are harmonious, or pleasing and peaceful. The use of contrasting colors can make paintings look active and aggressive.

Impressionist artists followed a rule that color was everything in a painting and that black, the non-color, must never appear. The Expressionists used black in a symbolic way. For instance, they used black to express feelings of despair or depression.

Light is also a determining factor in any composition. In analyzing a painting or drawing in terms of light it is interesting to note whether it is illuminated by its own

CARAVAGGIO. *The Conversion of Saint Paul.* 1600-01. Santa Maria del Popolo, Rome.
Artificial light, as used here by Caravaggio, comes from a point outside the composition and is focused on the most significant thematic point. This is divine light, emphasizing the artist's message. The figure of Saint Paul, receiving the Holy Spirit, is dramatically lit, as though on a stage.

light. This color/light combination is necessary for any composition, since both elements create order and space.

Lighting in paintings varies. Renaissance artists used intense light in the foreground, but diminished light in

CLAUDE MONET. *Rouen Cathedral–Morning.* 1894. Musée d'Orsay, Paris.
Light and color can capture a moment. This is imaginative use of color. The cathedral, with all its ornamental Gothic detail, offers ideal variations of light, which is suited to the study of the atmosphere it gives off. Monet was not really trying to paint the cathedral. Instead, he wanted to show, through a series of paintings, the different moods that surround it at different times of day.

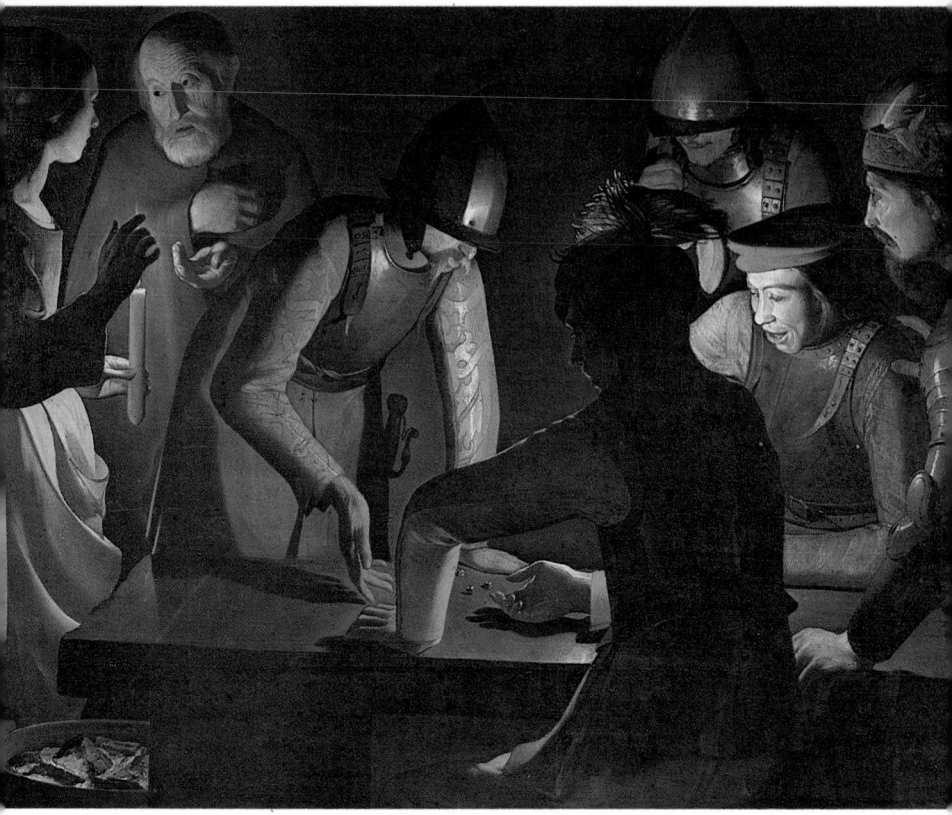

GEORGES DE LA TOUR. *The Denial of Saint Peter*. 1645. Nantes Museum, Nantes, France.
Natural light comes from a candle—a real, identifiable source. This is often the case with de la Tour. The technique is effective. It allows the artist to outline each element in the picture as a whole. It is a formal use of light, well suited to imaginative works such as this.

the background. This is in contrast to the gloom that is characteristic of Baroque works. In Baroque art, strongly lit figures emerged from a plain, dark background.

Light can also be used to separate the foreground, middle ground, and background of a painting, as in aerial perspective. Vermeer used dark foregrounds, with a maximum intensity of light in the background. Depending on how it is distributed, light can be all of the same kind, dual—in which dark backgrounds emphasize the figures—or mixed.

The light can come either from outside the picture or from an identifiable source, such as the candle in Georges de la Tour's *Denial of Saint Peter*. External light is used in a variety of ways in a composition. It can be focused or diffused, real or unreal, composite or purely conceptual.

JACOPO BASSANO. *Adoration of the Shepherds*. Second half of the 17th century. Her Majesty, The Queen's Collection. Hampton Court, London.
The light in this work is symbolic. It comes from the Christ Child and the angels above, and creates an interplay of light and dark. A similar use of light—from the angel above the tent—is found in Francesca's *The Dream of Constantine* on page 64.

GIOVANNI BELLINI. *Woman Combing Her Hair*. 1516. Kunsthistorisches Museum, Vienna, Austria. This late work seems, at first, to have a natural lighting effect, but that is not the case. The window in the background provides no light. It is just perspective space. The artist has abandoned logic and created a totally artificial balance of tones. What we have called pictorial reality is never a faithful representation of physical reality.

The use of light to create shadows is called **chiaroscuro**. The use of more dark area than light area is called **tenebrism**.

Tangible light comes from a light source within the picture—a candle, a torch or a lamp—which gives a logical chiaroscuro effect. Raphael and El Greco use this tangible light. Caravaggio, on the other hand, uses an external artificial light source, which throws light on one specific part of the composition.

Diffused light softens the outlines of objects. Some works of Leonardo da Vinci and the Italian artist Correggio illustrate this.

Real light, an almost impossible dream of the painter, has been sought by many artists. For example, Claude Lorrain, painting mostly in Italy during the 17th century, mixed his colors in the fields, matched them against the light effects he saw, and then rushed back to to his studio to work on his painting. The Impressionists completed works in the open air, all the time observing the effects of light and color. Throughout history, artists have tried to merge what they see with what they paint.

Religious painting, on the other hand, tends to use figures—the Christ Child, for example—as the source of symbolic light.

Light must be divided into two forms—artistic and conceptual. Artistic light includes all those forms we have discussed. Conceptual light tries to emphasize the message. By the use of light, artists draw attention to the particular area of the composition, which they want the viewer to concentrate. This use of light is best seen in the works of Caravaggio, who also emphasizes his realist message by using artificial light.

THÉODORE GÉRICAULT. *The Raft of the Medusa*. 1819. The Louvre, Paris.
The dramatic power of a painting stems from two basic factors—lighting, and the rhythm of the composition itself. Here the artist draws the viewer's attention to the two pieces of cloth, white and red, that the two figures in the top part of the painting are waving. From here, we can follow the whole structural rhythm of the work, based on one diagonal crossed by another (the great sail). Thus, a conflict is created between the desires of the survivors and fate, which seems to be pushing them away from salvation.

All works of art have areas of greater and lesser emphasis. Such areas are the beginning of a visual journey that will please the viewer if the distribution of space, color, and light are satisfactory.

The focal point of a painting, most often a figure, is usually the area of greatest contrast, both of tone and of color. The focal point, the rhythm of the composition, the color, and the light are the basis for understanding a work.

ANONYMOUS. *The Goddess Knut, Surrounded by Signs of the Zodiac.* 2nd century. British Museum, London.
Throughout the history of art, religious themes have always been important. Most civilizations have portrayed their gods. The Egyptians showed them in their tombs and coffins. Here we see Knut, wife of Geb. She is goddess of the heavens and is shown symbolically by the signs of the zodiac. If we do not recognize the character represented, our appreciation is limited to form alone, and the picture will lose some of its meaning.

SALVADOR DALI. *Christ of Saint John of the Cross.* 1951. Kelvingrove Art Gallery and Museum, Glasgow, Scotland.
Few artists have created religious art since the 19th century. An exception is Dali. This work belongs to the tradition of Spanish realist painting from earlier centuries. Starting from a very modern viewpoint, Dali tries to create a message from Spanish mystical literature. This shows how beliefs of the past can be reinterpreted in modern style. One message has many valid interpretations.

THE MEANING OF THE WORK

TINTORETTO. *Death of Holofernes.* 1555-79. Prado Museum, Madrid. A knowledge of the story is necessary for a full understanding of this picture. Both the Old and the New Testaments must be read to understand the religious painting of the Western world. Only if we have this knowledge can we judge whether a picture accurately portrays its message. Here we see an interpretation of the episode in the Old Testament of the Douay Bible when Judith, having called upon God, "took hold of the hair of his head . . . and smote [struck with a sword] twice upon his neck with all her might, and she took away his head from him." (Jth. 13:7-11)

A painting must be considered as a whole. In it, technique, composition, and content come together to form a work of art.

It is through technique and composition that artists express their beliefs—religious, nonreligious, cultural, or purely artistic. These are expressed visually by themes.

The history of art started with the magical, represented by the paintings of the prehistoric world. Prehistoric artists—primarily hunters—painted images

of animals they wished to capture for food and clothing. Their paintings represented possession, and sometimes their desires became reality. This magical influence surfaces throughout the whole history of art.

Sometimes art is simply decorative. Such art does not claim to be a copy of reality. Instead, real elements are gathered together into a composition which does not tell a story, but is simply an ornament. Such applied

BARTOLOMÉ ESTABAN MURILLO. *The Holy Family with a Bird*. 1650. Prado Museum, Madrid. Baroque art sentimentalized themes and brought them closer to everyday life. Religious art of the time often depicted saints. Joseph was one of those most frequently shown. This picture displays the realism with which religious themes were treated. At the same time, it shows Joseph as the leading player, with the Virgin Mary placed in the background.

art does not have any real message beyond pleasing the eye.

The major division in themes is between the religious and the secular, or nonreligious. Religious themes are found in the ancient cultures of Egypt, Assyria, Mesopotamia, Persia, and other countries. In very old works from these cultures, the theme mainly exists in sculpture. Paintings from ancient Greece and Rome are usually of secular subjects.

LLUÍS BORRASSÀ. *Resurrection*. 1411-18. Museum of Catalan Art, Barcelona.
The Gothic world placed great value on the symbolic element of a composition. Here, the figure of the risen Christ symbolizes the triumph of religion over paganism, which is represented by the sleeping soldiers. The composition itself is eloquent and fits the message of the picture.

Every portrayal of a religious event is interpreted in different ways. The interpretation depends on two things: who the artist is, and in what period of history the portrayal is done. An artist will often put religious figures in the clothing of his or her own time. This adds to the variety of ways a subject is treated. Medieval artists stressed the symbolic character of a person. Renaissance and Baroque artists sentimentalized the subject.

Baroque artists used the lives of the saints as examples of conduct to be imitated. It was the ability to inform

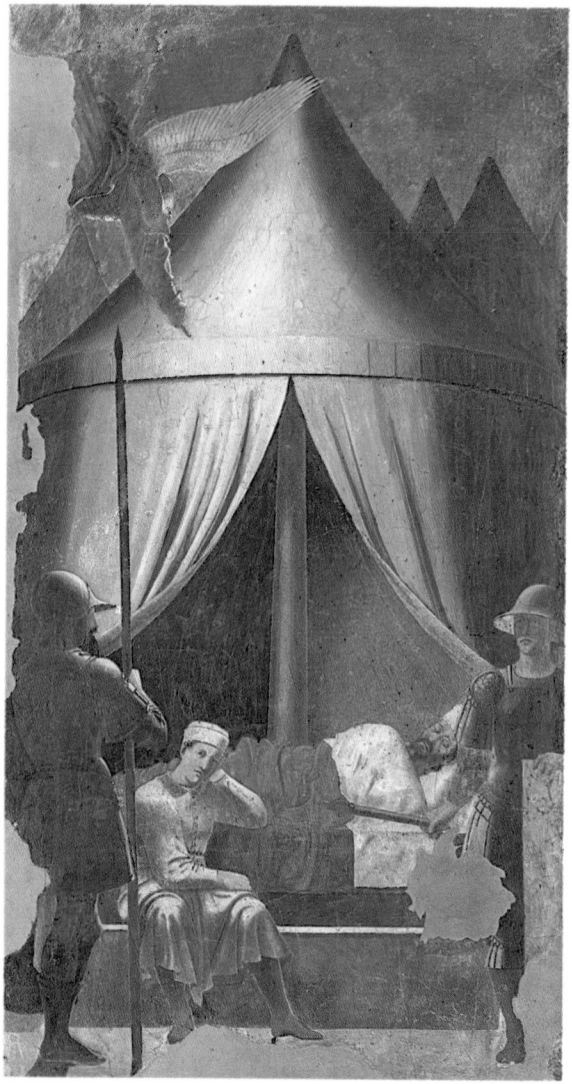

PIERO DELLA FRANCESCA. *The Dream of Constantine*. 1455. Church of San Francesco, Arezzo, Italy.
Piero della Francesca depicted the story of *The Dream of Constantine* very well on the walls of a church. The sleeping emperor dreams that an angel shows him a cross, and says "Under this sign shalt thou conquer."

JOSÉ ANTOLÍNEZ. *The Immaculate Conception.* 1670. Private Collection. The Virgin is one of the most widely portrayed themes in the history of art. Seventeenth-century artists made her the main figure in many paintings. The heavenly depiction of the figure raises it above the viewer and presents it as a cult object. The figure of the Holy Spirit symbolizes divine conception, and the white lilies represent purity.

and teach that made painting an important art form during the Baroque period.

The use of saints as perfect examples is a visual way of expressing the union of chosen souls with God. They are models to follow, ideals toward which to strive.

A list of all the main religious themes would be extensive. At various times, images from the New Testament have been linked to various saints. The Virgin Mary, surrounded by saints, was a common scene in works of the Renaissance period. During the Baroque period, artists introduced, as subject matter, the Immaculate Conception. At other times, religion has been linked to stories of real events—miracles, apparitions, or martyrdoms of the saints. Sometimes the Holy Trinity (Father, Son, and Holy Ghost), the Resurrection (of Christ), and the Eucharist

TITIAN. *Charles V at Mühlberg*. 1548. Prado Museum, Madrid. This is a portrait that has symbolic meaning. We see a physical likeness of the king but, above all, the picture symbolizes the Spanish Catholic monarchy triumphing over the Protestants on the banks of the Elbe.

(communion) are shown. There are many ways of depicting these subjects, and they often are interwoven into the same painting.

Understanding a religious painting depends on its visual attraction and on a recognition of its theme. Some knowledge of the Christian saints and of the Old

DAVID TENIERS. *Drinkers and Smokers.* 1660. Prado Museum, Madrid.
The depiction of scenes of everyday life reached its peak in 17th-century Flanders. Throughout the history of art, scenes of peasant, middle-class, and upper-class life have been the subjects of paintings in many different styles and interpretations. If we look carefully here, we can see a faithful reproduction of an atmosphere and of various levels of society.

JEAN-HONORÉ FRAGONARD. *The Abbot of Saint-Non.* 1769. Museum of Catalan Art, Barcelona.
Note here the harmony between the composition of the picture and the personality of the person portrayed. The zigzag layout is meant to show the arrogant character of Jean Claude-Richard de Saint-Non, the Abbot of Pothieres. The artist is not so much concerned with symbolism as with the depiction of a strong person, of someone sure of himself. Here, we see the portrayal of an attitude, not descriptive detail.

and New Testaments is essential for a complete understanding of such works.

Secular painting has many thematic styles. One is the portrait. The Romans introduced the idea of portraits into painting. However, few examples of their work have survived, and their portraiture, or portrait making, is best known through their sculptures. The use of portraits generally disappeared until Gothic times, when portraits and self-portraits became more commonplace. The basic aim of the portrait was to concentrate on a subject and the many ways in which it could be depicted.

This individual treatment of a subject includes the family group portrait. Another type of portrait, in which the subject is shown with the saints, was done in the Baroque period of the 17th century.

Genre painting depicts realistic scenes from everyday life. In 17th-century Holland, the middle class and

FRANÇOIS BOUCHER
***Miss O'Murphy*. 1752.**
Alte Pinakothek, Munich, West Germany.
We see here the distinction between a person posing for a portrait and a model posing for a pictorial composition. In this painting of Louise O'Murphy, a young girl of loose morals, Boucher reflected the tastes of a part of French society of the time. This single picture sums up an entire group.

PAUL CÉZANNE. *Still Life with Apples and Oranges*. 1885-1900. Musée d'Orsay, Paris. Still life has always had clear links with the society it depicts. Communities reflect daily life through the objects. After the 19th century, objects in such paintings became less symbolic.

VINCENT VAN GOGH. *Sunflowers*. 1888-89. Staat Gallerie, Munich. Flower paintings have both a decorative and a pictorial value. They represent both the courtly and the middle-class way of life. Flower painters tried to paint their subjects as faithfully as possible, paying great attention to detail. Gradually, they simplified these works. Van Gogh has merely suggested the forms of the sunflowers, using a thick layer of paint to give a feeling of their texture.

ANDRÉ DÉRAIN.
***Westminster Bridge*. 1905. Paris.**
This is a "pure" landscape, painted for its own sake, without figures. It is linked with the middle class. It appreciates what it represents. The countryside and the city frequently competed as subjects for paintings. The landscape is an intermediate stage between the realist works of the 17th century and the photography of the 20th century.

WILLIAM TURNER.
***Storm at Sea*. 1840. Tate Gallery, London.**
Here, Turner does not depict a seascape, but uses his canvas to portray a world of feelings. This is not a reflection of reality—it represents an imagined reality. It is painting in its purest form.

the aristocracy, or upper class, had themselves portrayed in their immediate surroundings so they could be depicted as they lived.

Still life is another theme. Together with flower painting, it came to prominence in the 16th and 17th centuries. It has a double role: It depicts a society and is a decoration. It has been one of the most popular themes during the last three centuries. Impressionist artists made it decorative, and Cubist artists used it as a vehicle for the study of forms.

Renaissance artists used landscapes as a complementary or perspective element. Landscape painting in its own right first appeared in central Europe. In the 17th century, Dutch painters, such as Hobbema, Ruysdael, and Vermeer, depicted the landscape in a realistic manner, as an expression of their sheer pleasure in the world around them. In Italy, the French artist Claude Lorrain used the landscape to capture a mood. The 18th-century artists in England made the landscape a theme.

DIEGO RIVERA. *Man at the Crossroads Looking with Hope and High Vision to the Choosing of a New and Better Future.* 1934. Palace of Fine Arts, Mexico City, Mexico. Rivera's mural commemorates the average citizen, daily life, and social change. Rivera was originally commissioned by Nelson Rockefeller in 1932 to paint this mural in New York City's RCA Building. Because Rivera included a portrait of Lenin, Rockefeller had the fresco destroyed before it was completely finished. Rivera re-created the mural in Mexico City on a wall donated by the Mexican government. This particular work depicted an ideal world that was controlled by educated workers. It was a world in which war, as well as religion, was superceded by socialist doctrines. This version of the mural contains portraits not only of Lenin, but also of Trotsky, Marx, Engels, and other communist figureheads.

Historical themes are related to myths. Paintings that record successful events or efforts are clearly linked to national pride.

Royalty and common people all want the events in which they were the winners to be remembered. Sometimes the desire for personal glory makes an individual the main figure in a work of art. After the Renaissance, this desire to be remembered became very strong and became more evident in artistic works. Use of a low horizon and symbolism increase the importance of the main figure in commemorative art.

PABLO PICASSO.
***Guernica*. 1936.**
Casón del Buen Retiro, Madrid.
Here, the desire to record an event is turned into an artistic subject of social judgment. Picasso depicts no glory, just the drama of war. Two aspects need to be pointed out: the mono-

Mythology has probably been the greatest art theme. It has two sides—religious and symbolic. In the ancient world and in Eastern cultures, mythical gods represented what Christian figures and events represent during the Middle Ages. The gods were used to illustrate a Christian message, but their use could vary. Historical and mythological art often carries an assumption that the viewer has a detailed knowledge of the subject.

Allegory, which has appeared in art from the beginning, is the representation of ideas, such as the

Immaculate Conception, virtue, vice, faith, charity, justice, strength, courage, and cowardice. It is linked to religious painting, but above all, to glorified historical figures. The virtues of the Christian hero are best represented in allegorical form.

Modern painters have experimented with form and have given us nonfigurative representations, which illustrate the purity of art. They have also given us form valid in itself, form with meaning. This can be called imaginative use of form. We should not seek to chrome, or one-color, nature of the picture, which tends to create a certain distance; and the scorn of a dictator, here represented as the executioner of a confused town. When a Nazi official asked who had done the preliminary sketches for *Guernica*, Picasso replied, "You did."

JOAN MIRÓ. *Woman and Birds at Dawn.* 1946. Fundacio Miró, Barcelona.
Miró is a great believer of significant form, a symbolism not easily understood. He moved away from the established language of reality and form, then created his own language within a set of his own rules. The viewer who does not understand Miró's paintings should remember that a person who does not read Chinese will not understand something written in that language. The message is clear, however, to those who do know Chinese.

identify form with reality, but to judge it in its own right.

Painting can only be understood in the framework of culture and thought. This is both its great virtue and its great limitation.

FRANCISCO DE GOYA. *Saturn Devouring His Son.* 1819. Prado Museum, Madrid.
For Goya, the theme here portrays the decadence of a set of social values in which he had once believed. Saturn represents unlimited power, capable of destroying—without feeling—beings whom he himself had created and protected. Spain, in the 19th century, appeared this way to Goya, and he depicted his disillusionment in a thinly veiled disguise.

ART THROUGHOUT THE AGES

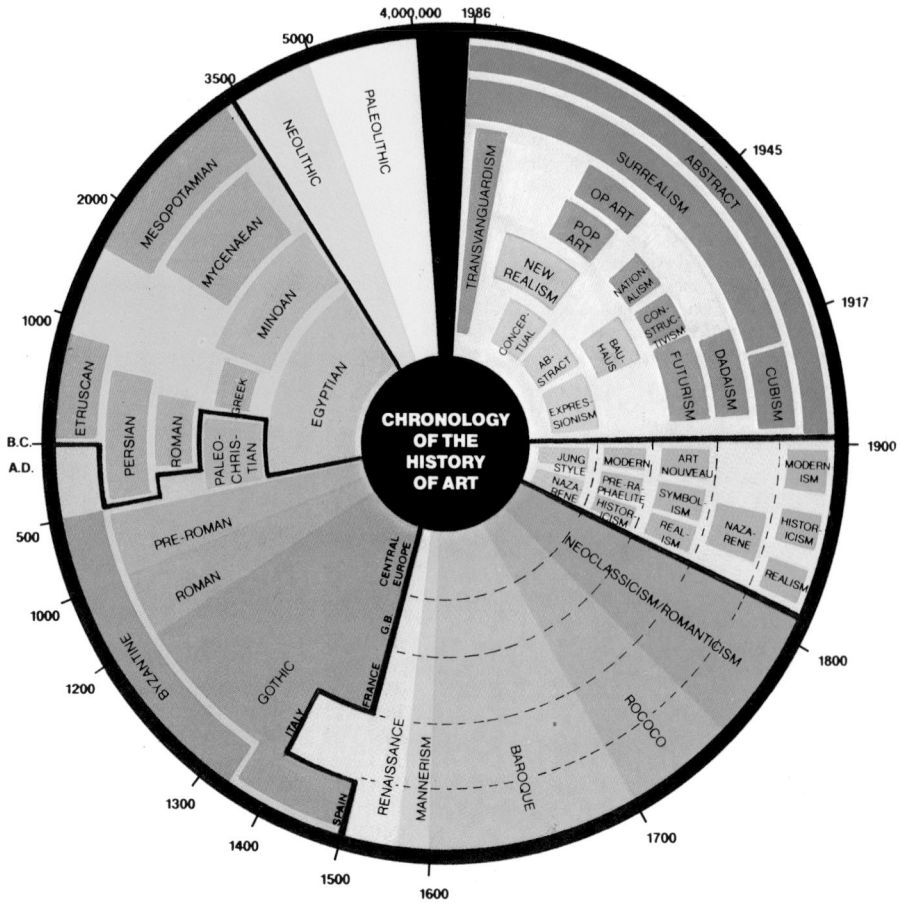

This chart shows the evolution of Western and Near Eastern art through the ages. The terms are those that art historians traditionally use to label periods of time in various cultures where definite stylistic tendencies have occurred. The books in the Key to Art series examine the interplay of artists, ideas, methods, and cultural influences that have affected the evolution of specific art styles.

INDEX OF ILLUSTRATIONS

ANONYMOUS: *Baptism of Christ* 24
Beatus of Cardeña 13
Casa Masferrer Sgraffiti 18
Christ and the Apostles 40
Christ of Saint Clement of Taüll 13
The Goddess Knut, Surrounded by Signs of the Zodiac 60
Large Bison with Straight Tail 11
The Martyrdom of Saint Andrew 4-5
Nativity, Side altar in Sagas, Solsona 33
Oxen Trampling Grain 35
Proculus the Baker and His Wife 17
ANGELICO, Fra: *The Annunciation* 15
ANTOLÍNEZ, José: *The Immaculate Conception* 65
BASSANO, Francesco: *Adoration of the Shepherds* 57
BELLINI, Giovanni: *Woman Combing Her Hair* 58
BORRASSÀ, Lluís: *Resurrection* 63
BOUCHER, François: *Miss O'Murphy* 68
CANAL, Antonio: *View of the Church of the Salute and Entrance to the Grand Canal* 38
CANALETTO: see **CANAL, Antonio**
CARAVAGGIO: see **MERISI, Michelangelo**
CÉZANNE, Paul: *The Card Players* 3
Still Life with Apples and Oranges 69
DALI, Salvador: *Christ of Saint John of the Cross* 60
DEGAS, Edgar: *Glass of Absinthe* 49
La Toilette 45
DELLA FRANCESCA, Piero: see **PIERO DELLA FRANCESCA**
DERAIN, André: *Westminster Bridge* 70
DÜRER, Albrecht: *Tools to Duplicate Perspective*, engraving 37
FERNÁNDEZ, Alejo: *The Virgin of the Navigators*, outline 35
FORTUNY, Mariano: *The Spanish Wedding* 28-29
FRAGONARD, Jean-Honoré: *The Abbot of Saint-Non* 67
GÉRICAULT, Théodore: *The Raft of the Medusa* 59
GOYA, Francisco de: *Saturn Devouring His Son* 77
GOZZOLI, Benozzo: *Procession of the Magi* 6-7
GRECO, El: see **THEOTOKÓPOULOS, Doménikos**
HALS, Frans: *The Gypsy* 26
HAMEN, Juan van der: *Still Life*, outline 45
LÉGER, Ferdinand: *Homage to Jacques-Louis David*, outline 25
MANET, Édouard: *Déjeuner sur l'Herbe* 12
MASACCIO: *The Expulsion from Paradise* 16
MASACCIO/MASOLINO: *The Virgin and Child with Saint Anne* 43
MAZZOLA, Francesco: *The Madonna with the Long Neck*, outline 32
MERISI, Michelango: *The Conversion of Saint Paul* 54
MILLARES, Manolo: *Manikin* 21
MILLET, Jean-François: *El Angelus* 53
MIRÓ, Joan: *Woman and Birds at Dawn* 76
MONET, Claude: *Rouen Cathedral–Morning* 55
MUNCH, Edvard: *The Scream* 31
MURILLO, Bartolomé Esteban: *The Holy Family with a Bird* 62
PARET Y ALCÁZAR, Luis: *The Go-Between and the Lovers* 22
PARMIGIANINO: see **MAZZOLA, Francesco**
PERGUGINO: see **VANNUCCI, Pietro**
PICASSO, Pablo:
Guernica 74-75
The Maids of Honor (Las Meninas) 36
PIERO DELLA FRANCESCA: *Baptism of Christ*, outline 50
Alterpiece of Brera, outline 50
The Dream of Constantine 64
POLLOCK, Jackson: *No. 32* 27
POUSSIN, Nicolas: *The Rape of the Sabines*, outline 42
POZZO, Andrea: *False Cupolo* 39
RAPHAEL: *The School of Athens*, outline 34
RIVERA, Diego: *Man at the Crossroads Looking with Hope and High Vision to the Choosing of a New and Better Future* 72-73
REYMERSWAELE, Marinus: *The Money Changer and His Wife* 10
ROBUSTI, Jacopo: *The Washing of the Feet* 41
Death of Holofernes 61
RUBENS, Peter Paul: *The Three Graces* 30
Rustic Dance 44
The Raising of the Cross, outline 46
Hélène Fourment and Her Children, outline 48
SÁNCHEZ COTÁN, Juan: *Still Life*, outline 48
SIGNORELLI, Luca: *Holy Family* 47
TÁPIES, Antoni: *Grafitti* 20
TENIERS, David: *Drinkers and Smokers* 67
THEOTOKÓPOULOS, Doméniko: *Laocoön* 51
TINTORETTO: see **ROBUSTI, Jacopo**
TITIAN: see **TIZIANO VECELLIO**
TIZIANO VECELLIO: *Charles V at Mühlberg* 66
TOUR, Georges de la: *The Denial of Saint Peter* 56
TOUR, Maurice-Quentin de la: *Portrait of Madame Pompadour* 23
TRAMULLES, Manuel: *The Concert* 14
TURNER, William: *Storm at Sea* 70-71
VAN EYCK, Jan: *The Arnolfini Marriage* 19
VAN GOGH, Vincent: *Self Portrait with Hat* 52
Sunflowers 69
VANNUCCI, Pietro: *The Delivery of the Keys*, outline 41
The Virgin and Child with Four Saints, outline 46
VELÁZQUEZ, Diego:
The Maids of Honor (Las Meninas) 36
VERMEER VAN DELFT, Jan: *View of Delft* 8
VON ES, Rudolf: *Nativity*, outline 48
WATTEAU, Antoine: *Gilles* 43
ZURBARÁN, Francisco: *Still Life*, outline 42

CONTENTS

Introduction 3
The Artist's Tools 9
Supports Used 11
Techniques 15
The Elements of Form 25
The Structure of a Work 33
The Meaning of the Work 61
Art Throughout the Ages 78
Index of Illustrations 79

ACKNOWLEDGMENTS

Aisa: pp. 28-29, 74-75; Alte Pinakothek, Munich: p.68; A.P.: pp. 11, 24, 35, 60; Association of National Museums: pp. 3, 12, 38, 43, 55, 59, 69, 70; F. Catalá-Roca: p. 18; Fundació Miró, Barcelona: p. 76; Giraudon: p. 23, 45, 49, 56, 69; Glasgow Museum and Art Galleries, Glasgow: p. 60; I.G.D.A.: p. 53; Index: pp. 4-5, 13, 33; Kunsthistorisches Museum, Vienna: p. 58; Museum of Catalan Art, Barcelona: pp. 13, 40, 63; Museum of Modern Art, Barcelona: p. 14; National Gallery, Oslo: p. 31; The National Gallery, London: p. 19; Oronoz: pp. 26, 32, 51, 52; Picasso Museum, Barcelona: p. 36; Pollock-Krasner Foundation/ARS, N.Y.: p.27; Prado Museum, Madrid: pp. 10, 15, 30, 36, 42, 44, 57, 61, 62, 66, 67, 77; Desmond Rochfort: p. 72-73; Scala: p. 6-7, 8, 16, 17, 39, 47, 54, 64; The Tate Gallery, London: p. 70-71; Juan-Ramón Triadó: p. 20, 21.